How Families Work Together

Mary Whiteside, Ph.D
with Craig E. Aronoff, Ph.D. and John L. Ward, Ph.D.

Family Business Leadership Series, No. 4

Family Enterprise Publishers
P.O. Box 4356
Marietta, GA 30061-4356

ISSN: 1071-5010
ISBN: 0-9651011-4-2
© 1993
Fifth Printing

Family Business Leadership Series

We believe that family businesses are special, not only to the families that own and manage them but to our society and to the private enterprise system. Having worked and interacted with hundreds of family enterprises in the past twenty years, we offer the insights of that experience and the collected wisdom of the world's best and most successful family firms.

This volume is a part of a series offering practical guidance for family businesses seeking to manage the special challenges and opportunities confronting them.

To order additional copies, contact:
Family Enterprise Publishers
1220-B Kennestone Circle
Marietta, Georgia 30066
Tel: 1-800-551-0633
Web Site: www.efamilybusiness.com

Quantity discounts are available.

Other volumes in the series include:

Family Business Succession: The Final Test of Greatness, 2nd ed.
Family Meetings: How to Build a Stronger Family and a Stronger Business, 2nd ed.
Another Kind of Hero: Preparing Successors for Leadership
Family Business Compensation
How to Choose and Use Advisors: Getting the Best Professional Family Business Advice
Financing Transitions: Managing Capital and Liquidity in the Family Business
Family Business Governance: Maximizing Family and Business Potential
Preparing Your Family Business for Strategic Change
Making Sibling Teams Work: The Next Generation
Developing Family Business Policies: Your Guide to the Future
Family Business Values: How to Assure a Legacy of Continuity and Success
More Than Family: Non-Family Executives in the Family Business
Make Change Your Family Business Tradition
Family Business Ownership: How To Be An Effective Shareholder
Conflict and Communication in the Family Business
Letting Go: Preparing Yourself to Relinquish Control of the Family Business
Nurturing the Talent to Nurture the Legacy: Career Development in the Family Business
Working for a Family Business: A Non-Family Employee's Guide to Success

Contents

Tables and Exhibits

I. *How Family Shapes the Future of Your Business*

Nothing is as precious — or as complicated — as family.

After years of work together in the family printing business, members of the Smith family, a close and loving clan, are about to learn that principle anew as they gather for their first family meeting.

The candles have just cooled on a surprise 59th-birthday cake for John Smith, founder of Smith Printing, when he makes his announcement: After 37 years as head of the business, John will retire in a year. He has long dreamed that his children, Rob and Kathy, would take over the business. And he is looking forward to a vacation from the day-to-day pressures of managing the company.

Yet as John sits at the head of the company conference room talking about his heartfelt plans for his children and his company, an uneasy feeling creeps into the pit of his stomach. He had hoped that his children would respond enthusiastically. But while his daughter Kathy, a 33-year-old Duke MBA who has sparked fast growth as Smith Printing's vice president of marketing, is excited and bursting with questions, the session is in grave danger of stalling on the silence of son Rob.

As Smith Printing's finance VP, Rob bypassed a chance nine years earlier to set up his own accounting practice so he could create the financial-reporting systems Smith Printing needed to survive a recession and grow. But Rob, now 35, has never expressed an interest in leading the company. Instead, the plans John is setting forth now — for shared second-generation family leadership with Rob as the new CEO — seem to depress him.

Though John hasn't said much about Rob's reticence in the past, his son's silence is rapidly becoming too obvious to ignore. Why is Rob so quiet? John wonders. And what does it mean for the family and the business?

■

A strong, cohesive family brings a multitude of potential strengths to a business.

Business families often enjoy a sense of shared identity. They benefit from common interests and a shared "language," including private expressions, mannerisms and communication styles. Family members know much about each other's strengths and weaknesses, and they have abundant opportunities to support each other. They have the satisfaction

1

of learning together about each other and the business. Ideally, they share common values and a sense of mission and purpose.

Even more powerful but less understood, families share a multi-generational history of ancestors, events and relationships. That history conveys potent behavioral patterns that influence the present and future. These ways of perceiving, feeling and behaving are woven even more deeply into the fabric of family legacy than nationality, ethnicity or creed. Any time a business family reaches a point of significant stress or reorganization, as the Smiths have, these family patterns can surface in significant ways.

The Smiths, a composite family created from our experiences with actual business families, don't know it yet, but the transition John has set in motion with his announcement will lead them to a deeper respect and understanding of the power and value of the rich family legacy they share.

A Tool for Achievement. That's what this booklet is about: how families work together. Like other booklets in **The Family Business Leadership Series**, it is a tool to help members of business families achieve a common purpose. By following the Smiths and other families through some typical experiences, it offers help in recognizing and understanding some of the patterns common in business families' heritage. Though the examples we cite in this booklet are based on the experiences of real families, none of them are actual families, and resemblance to any actual family is accidental. Nevertheless, the principles offered are intended to help all kinds of families make the most of their experience together.

The pages that follow examine how the workings of a family can affect a business. The booklet discusses the characteristics of normal families. It lays out the basics of "family systems theory," including its central idea of wholeness — that each family is a unique and emotionally meaningful unit with its own structure, beliefs, patterns of relating and ways of dealing with stress. Just as important, it shows how those patterns can reverberate through the generations, affecting the lives and work of sons and daughters, grandchildren and beyond.

Bringing About Change. The booklet shows how to tap the power of a rich family history and heritage to accomplish shared goals. It offers simple tools for improving relations, from writing a code of conduct to practicing effective communication skills. And it shows how to plant the seeds of change *by example* — by changing one's own behavior in a way that encourages others to work together more productively.

The booklet also offers help in interpreting trouble signs in family relations. It explains the role of the family professional in helping all kinds of families to reach their goals. *Perhaps most important, it offers some keys to setting in motion a family process aimed at learning and growing together.*

This process may take many forms. Studying good communication techniques as a group; attending family business seminars and forums; or reading and discussing as a family writings like this one or others mentioned in the "Suggested Reading" list at the back of this booklet, can all be helpful. For larger families, inviting a family business consultant to speak on the dynamics of business families can be effective.

Some families use the family meeting as a vehicle for learning, including items relating to their family's unique strengths or values on family-meeting agendas. (Family meetings are discussed in depth in No. 2 of **The Family Business Leadership Series**, *Family Meetings: How to Build a Stronger Family and a Stronger Business*.) Others find that preparing a family mission statement leads them into a discussion of family patterns of achievement or values. Some families also find it helpful to write a family history or construct and study a genogram, a kind of information-rich family tree that is discussed in detail later in this volume. As families study their legacy together, they often learn much about their own dynamics and the powerful family patterns that so strongly influence them.

II. *Business vs. Family: Crossing the Chinese Wall*

Why should business families be concerned with the workings of the family? Shouldn't business and family issues be kept separate?

Indeed, the cultures of family and business can be nearly opposite. Business thinking at its best is a more disciplined, manageable process than, say, anticipating the needs of a child, organizing a family outing or selecting a mate. Many business owners see great benefit in rigorously separating the two realms.

Yet the Chinese Wall between family and business rapidly crumbles when these same business owners begin talking about their most deeply felt life purposes and rewards. When they share goals and values for the business, family plays a central role. Many see the involvement of the family in the business as their greatest single source of satisfaction (or sometimes, pain). "Having my family work with me and continue the business has been the greatest payoff for a lifetime of hard work," some owner-managers say.

These same business owners often treat family ownership as a business asset. Many point to it as an emblem of quality. A company's advertising may boast that "our family has been making chocolate for over 100 years," connoting experience and cohesiveness of management. Indeed, a strong family's common goals, values and shared sense of belonging can be rich, fortifying soil in which to plant a business strategy. Though "kinship" is a word that is seldom used today, its meaning in the past — of a bond that is constantly strengthening and reinforcing individuals, assigning them value and fortifying their patterns of working together — is a paradigm for today's healthy management culture.

Crucial areas of family and business planning are wound in a Gordian knot. Estate and strategic planning are interwoven with succession and personal financial planning, raising issues of inheritance, justice, entitlement and equity in both family and business realms. And, as we shall see in Rob Smith's case, personal career plans can become deeply entangled with the needs of the family business.

Family business ownership means that family members share the same economic destiny, riding the peaks and troughs of the business's fortunes together. And family history in turn leaves a deep mark on the business. Because so many of the people working in a family business share the same family history, the business is more deeply affected than non-family firms by employees' ways of thinking, acting and relating to each other. (See Figure 1.)

5

FIGURE 1

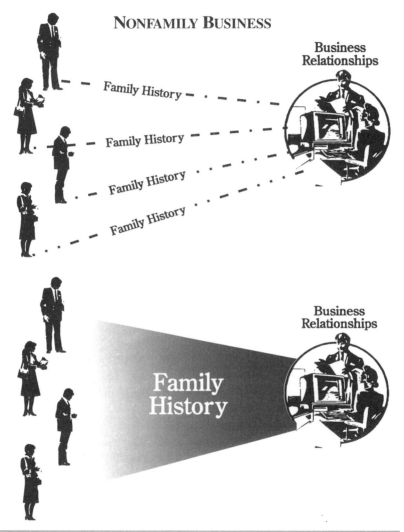

How Employees' Family History Affects the Business

NONFAMILY BUSINESS

A growing number of business owners are acknowledging the powerful relationship between business and family and working to integrate the two in the most productive way possible (see Table 1). As discussed below,

6

TABLE 1

THE TIES THAT BIND:
INTERRELATIONSHIPS BETWEEN THE FAMILY BUSINESS AND THE BUSINESS FAMILY

- Family plays role in ownership purposes and goals

- Family ownership seen as business asset

- Business benefits from family members' loyalty and productivity

- Family values and mission can be a business resource

- Shared family history colors management culture

- Business unites family in a shared economic destiny

- Overlapping interpersonal roles create intense and stressful business relationships

- Business and personal family planning overlap

building an understanding of how families work can speed this process, creating new synergies that can benefit both business and family.

■

As a manager, John Smith is frustrated to see his son Rob so withdrawn. John has always treated Rob well in the business, rewarded his accomplishments and tried to expand his opportunities. Now he is offering Rob what seems to him the business opportunity of a lifetime. Yet his son isn't responding. As a father, John feels a pang of concern.

What John does not know is that Rob's dream of starting his own accounting practice, though deferred by the demands of the family business, is still alive. With the family business running smoothly, Rob had decided a couple of weeks ago to discuss the issue with his father. Now, it seems, it is too late. Like George Bailey in the classic film, "It's a Wonderful Life," Rob feels his personal dreams are doomed forever to take a back seat to the family business.

John also has concerns about Kathy. Unlike her older brother, Kathy sees a role in the family business as a dream come true. As the younger child and a female, Kathy has strived long and hard to win her father's approval. In earning high honors at Duke in marketing, viewed by John as a man's field, she hoped her father would feel more comfortable in giving her responsibility in the business. When she expanded the company's marketing efforts to include more corporations in need of annual reports and other documents, the result was a 20 percent jump in output. For Kathy, her father's expression of delight and pride was as great a reward as her own self-satisfaction. Though Kathy's dream would have been to become CEO herself, she has accepted the likelihood that leadership of the business will be shared with her brother.

As a manager, John values Kathy's abilities and is delighted to see her so enthusiastic about succession. But as a father, he is concerned that she may be taking on too much. Kathy and her husband have both said in the past that they would like to have children at some point, yet Kathy seems heedless of that hope in her eager plans to expand the business. John finds himself wishing for grandchildren, and he can't help but wonder what Kathy is thinking these days about having a family.

■

III. *The Payoff: Understanding Family Patterns as a Collective Resource*

**The life which is unexamined
is not worth living.**

— Plato

What is the point of delving into the workings of the family?

Understanding how the family works has many of the same advantages as understanding how the human body works. It enables one to appreciate the value of good health. It helps avoid being victimized by unknown forces or influences. It helps to identify hereditary tendencies that can affect the body's welfare. And it helps the individual to explore new ways to function within the body.

For a family, a joint effort to understand how families work can be a powerful vehicle for appreciating strengths and values, for change and for growth. This self-study process can help family members cultivate positive attributes and develop greater appreciation and tolerance for each other. It can bring family members closer, affording them new joys and rewards in working together. It can help members be calmer and less threatened by family conflicts. It can free the family to enjoy more humor to leaven their relationships. Above all, it can cultivate empathy — a capacity for understanding and appreciating each other both as a family unit, and as individual products of the same family unit.

Freedom from Undesirable Patterns of the Past. Changing problem behaviors in families is far easier than most people think. Family behaviors that impede growth — poor communications, controlling behavior, pressure for unnecessary conformity and so on — are often rooted in powerful and *unconscious* family patterns of the past.

The power of family legacy has perhaps

Understanding how the family works has many of the same advantages as understanding how the human body works.

9

been most fully recognized by anthropologists such as Margaret Mead, who suggested that the smallest meaningful unit of analysis in the human family is five generations. A growing number of business families, mindful of these intergenerational bonds, are trying to preserve the most constructive aspects of their legacy, tapping grandparents as mentors and encouraging oral histories and other family endeavors.

An even more thorough look at all dimensions of the family's legacy can pay added dividends. **Many of the multigenerational patterns that powerfully influence family members' behavior are largely unconscious. When such patterns are outside the realm of family members' awareness, their power is vastly increased. When people are unaware of influences from the past, they cannot recognize choices or opportunities for change. They are more likely to be trapped in old patterns.**

These patterns can be positive. Some families exhibit multigenerational patterns of success, with generation after generation of high-achieving and satisfied individuals. Siblings through the generations may show a strong pattern of teamwork. Parents may tend in generation after generation to support children effectively in their efforts to become independent. Women in a family may enjoy a pattern of family support, encouragement and recognition for their professional accomplishments. Some families may display a continuing ability to pass on a cherished legacy, such as a business or property, perhaps increasing its value through the generations. Others may reliably help each other through troubled times.

For others, the patterns of the past are constraining or even destructive. Attitudes about expressing ourselves or dealing with conflict are handed down from generation to generation. Divorces or destructive relationships between parents and children or brothers and sisters can seem almost genetically transmitted in some families. In one example, each generation in a family founded and developed a successful business, only to have their children break off in pain and conflict to start their own businesses. This pattern is now in at least its fourth generation, which hopes to break the mold so that a family enterprise will have the advantage of multigenerational development.

Similarly, the offspring of a family of overachievers with one "black sheep" may unconsciously recreate the same set of relationships

When people are unaware of influences from the past, they cannot recognize choices or opportunities for change.

in their own families. Symptoms of emotional pain, such as alcoholism, incest, violence and suicide, also tend to be repeated in families from generation to generation. When allowed to remain behind the veil of family unconsciousness, such patterns can continue to shape relationships and affect even the most successful family business.

The best way to use family patterns to advantage — and to dissipate the power of problem patterns — is to learn about them. Building recognition and understanding affords family members incalculable gifts: greater control over their behavior, and greater opportunity to live the lives of their choice. Just as the evil dwarf in the fairy tale "Rumpelstiltskin" lost his power after the heroine was able to name him, negative patterns in the family legacy lose their power after they are recognized, acknowledged and "named."

IV. The "Normal" Family: A Dynamic and Powerful Unit

As one who left his father's farm at the age of 18, John Smith is proud to have created what he sees as a "family business." He is pleased that his own son Rob at 35 is still working by his side. And he is proud that he has built a substantial legacy for Rob and Kathy to share. The energy, shared values and cohesiveness of a close family can be a tremendous resource for a business, John believes.

Yet he is taken aback by the powerful reactions his retirement decision creates throughout the family, as well as the business. His wife Dorothy seems anxious and reluctant to discuss any aspect of his retirement. Kathy is plunging into long-term business planning, although her husband Ken looks increasingly uncomfortable as she plans to assume debt to partially buy out her father. Rob seems increasingly depressed and withdrawn. And Kathy and Rob, rather than showing the teamwork John had expected, seem uncharacteristically inclined to squabble.

■

If family dynamics are a rich tapestry of past and present patterns, what do the day-to-day interactions of a normal family look like?

Perhaps *not* as you might expect — if you expect to see uninterrupted peace, equality and harmony.

Normal families have arguments. In their experience, it's not bad to get into arguments — it's how you get out of them that counts. Nor do normal families avoid criticism of one another. In one study, researchers compared families of delinquent adolescent boys with families of normal teenagers. They found that while both groups of families had disagreements, negative exchanges and criticism, the families of healthy youngsters had a far higher frequency of positive communications than negative ones. Thus negative communications are normal and healthy, providing they are accompanied by frequent positive, constructive exchanges. **Particularly in times of stress, members of any normal family may experience lapses in communication, anxiety, conflict and a wide range of other problems in functioning together. A normal family understands this and is not afraid to acknowledge problems.**

Normal families are neither permissive nor unbending. Rather, they strike a balance between flexibility and stability. They can adapt to change without allowing chaos. And they can adhere to shared principles and practices without being rigid.

**Nor do normal families necessarily treat everyone equally —
though they *do* make their criteria for treatment fair, just and explicit.** One business family decided to devote most of its financial resources to the business. This would deeply affect the financial future of family members not working in the business, and family leaders made that clear.

Family members were encouraged to decide on their own, free of pressure or coercion, whether to work in the business. Those who chose to do so were given ample opportunity to build sweat equity and to advance their careers. "These are the resources we have," family leaders said. "You can take advantage of these resources if you are part of the business."

Those who chose not to work in the business were supported in their decision, but told they would receive less financial support and a smaller inheritance. "It's perfectly OK not to be in the business, and we fully support your decision either way. But you need to know that your choice will affect your financial participation in the family's resources."

While this message stirred a lot of feelings among family members, it also freed them to take responsibility for their own decisions. And it created a climate where strong family relationships could thrive, either inside or outside the business.

Here are a few additional characteristics of normal families, as described by J. S. Lewis and other authors of *No Single Thread: Psychological Health in Family Systems* (New York: Brunner/Mazel, 1976):

Healthy families aren't preoccupied with their own structure — that is, who has more power, who has the strongest relationships and so on. **Rather, power is shared and members' greatest concern is functioning well and accomplishing shared goals.** They emphasize cooperativeness, good humor and effectiveness.

These families welcome contact with new ideas and suggestions, though they examine and evaluate them all. Freedom in communicating is stressed. A need for intimacy isn't seen as weakness. Anger is accepted and affirmed as a sign that something needs to be changed or corrected — not as a problem that needs to be repressed or punished.

Healthy families aren't threatened by changes in direction. They acknowledge and adapt to change, separation or loss.

Normal families have arguments. In their experience, it's not bad to get into arguments — it's how you get out of them that counts.

Members acknowledge that making mistakes is natural, and each is allowed to fail without losing face or developing a negative self-image. Members can express their individual feelings and needs, and they are empathetic with others. And they have realistic expectations about others' ability to meet or fulfill their individual needs.

Members are receptive to each others' input and respect it. They enjoy negotiating with each other, and each is encouraged to develop skill in negotiation. Ambivalence is acceptable, and agreement results from inventive compromise. Even the smallest children are considered capable of contributing. While children are less powerful than adults, their contributions usually influence family decisions. Each child is guided and directed, and family rules are enforced without threats or intimidation.

In the Smiths' case, the disorientation and nascent conflict they are experiencing is perfectly normal to a family facing major change. A major test, however, will be how the Smiths choose to get through the change. Family members will need to communicate well and draw upon reserves of collective strength. Like many families, the Smiths are inclined to "protect" each other from conflict. Fortunately, they share common values and a foundation of trust — as well as a legacy of hard work, teamwork and a love for the business that they will soon discover together.

V. How the Family Works as a System

> **sys-tem:** *a regularly interacting or interdependent group of items forming a unified whole; a group of interacting bodies under the influence of related forces. (Webster's Seventh New Collegiate Dictionary, G.&C. Merriam Co., 1965).*

All of the traits of normal families discussed so far have a common feature: they address how individuals within families interact and affect each other. This quality of interrelatedness has given rise in recent decades to a whole new body of thought regarding how the family works as a system. In this section, we will discuss how some of these basic concepts can be useful to business families: triangles, differentiation of self, family structure, boundaries, family roles and emotional cutoff, as well as the use of genograms as a tool for learning.

In the past, psychological analysis focused on the individual as the emotionally meaningful unit. The family was seen as having meaning as a collection of related individuals. But beginning in the 1950s and continuing with increasing momentum to the present, professionals also have begun studying families themselves as a unit.

The central idea in this way of thinking, called "family systems theory," is that of wholeness — that **the family is a whole and unique unit with its own structure, beliefs and patterns of relating.** This approach sees the family group operating as an open, dynamic system. Each family has a unique style, cultural requirements, role relationships and rules, or ways of dealing with stress and expressing emotions.

Central Organizing Principles. Family members also may share central organizing principles or assumptions, termed by psychologist David Reiss "family paradigms." These central principles reflect the essence of a family's shared world view or attitude toward themselves and how they relate to the outside world. These constructs are influenced by social context. For example, Anglo-American families

> *Each family has a unique style, cultural requirements, role relationships and rules, or ways of dealing with stress and expressing emotions.*

17

in the United States are likely to value individual effort and the freedom to question authority. Mexican families are likely to value working cooperatively within the family and larger community, and expect respectful deference to authority. Within cultures, families' assumptions differ in many important ways. One family will see the world as ordered, predictable, and masterable. Another family will see its world as unstable, unpredictable, and potentially dangerous. Some families have a vivid experience of their own history as a central reference point. Others live in the present with little reference to the past. Such assumptions are shared by all family members and are seen in their patterns of actions with one another and with the outside world. When a family experiences a crisis, the family paradigm provides a way of explaining and understanding their experience and provides implicit guidelines for dealing with the crisis.

Individual Freedom within the Family. The influence of family culture on individual behavior is as invisible as that of any shaping organizational influence. We are unaware of the power of our everyday patterns until we step into a contrasting culture or until something interrupts or challenges our usual expectations. However, it is important to note that **family members can learn new behaviors. Each individual has free will to depart from family patterns. Nevertheless, in times of anxiety, family patterns have a strong tendency to take over.** Learning about family systems can help people understand these trigger points and choose logical, effective ways of dealing with stress.

Just as learning about management systems makes it easier to understand why a company is or isn't reaching its goals, learning about family systems can clarify and demystify the tension, obstacles and communication problems affecting a family. It enables family members to step back from individual relationships and see the family as a unit that is deeply marked both by individuals within it and by the generations that have gone before.

Thus the family is not just a collection of related individuals, but an emotionally meaningful unit. The whole is greater than the sum of the parts — the individuals that make up the family. Each individual's behavior and makeup simultaneously reflect the influence of the family system, and in turn influence that system. **Patterns within**

Each individual has free will to depart from family patterns. Nevertheless, in times of anxiety, family patterns have a strong tendency to take over.

the family are drawn from those of past generations and lay a foundation for the generations to come.

Family systems theory also maintains that unusual or abnormal behaviors in any member of a family can be related to problems within the intricately balanced family organization. Indeed, family systems theory began, in part, with the observation that schizophrenics who showed meaningful recovery when placed in treatment away from their families were likely to regress significantly when returned to their original family setting. Thus it was recognized that pain in one family member was sometimes tolerated and even inadvertently encouraged by the rest of the family, and that relationships among family members should be a central focus of behavioral therapy. It was also recognized that primary family relationships can act as a valuable healing resource.

Family therapy — as distinguished from individual therapy — has now gained wide acceptance and is widely taught and practiced. Underlying it are the principles espoused by Dr. Murray Bowen, M.D., one of the pioneers in family systems theory whose views are particularly applicable to family business, as described in his book *Family Therapy in Clinical Practice* (New York: Aronson, 1978). Many families find Dr. Bowen's principles applicable to their experience in business together, partly because his work stresses the importance of each person's taking responsibility for himself or herself in relationships. Many of the concepts and ideas discussed here arise from his work.

Triangles: Stabilizing Uncomfortable Relationships

As Rob Smith and his sister Kathy begin to lay plans for shared leadership of Smith Printing, conflicts arise in their usually harmonious relationship. Kathy wants to borrow money to invest in her idea for enhancing graphics production. Rob, concerned that the company will become too heavily leveraged too soon after a management change, presses for more self-financed growth.

In the past the siblings might have gone to John for advice. But neither Kathy nor Rob wants to go to do that at this stage, believing they should settle their differences themselves. Kathy's frustration soon spills out in a casual conversation with Dorothy. "Rob just isn't able to give fair consideration to my ideas," she complains. "I think he still thinks of me as his little sister."

Concerned, Dorothy invites Rob over to dinner, where she probes his feelings about working with Kathy, expresses her support and tries to smooth things over. Rob appreciates his mother's efforts and feels somewhat relieved after venting his frustrations to her. But when he leaves, he resolves to avoid dealing with Kathy as much as possible.

■

According to Bowen, *triangulation* is a basic process occurring in all families and other social groups. He observes that, under stress, a two-person relationship will form a three-person system. For example, tension might arise between a husband and a wife. The one who is most uncomfortable can relieve tension by "triangling in" a third person, perhaps by complaining about their son. Then the tension will shift to the parent-child twosome, relieving tension between the spouses. But the child, once he becomes drawn in, may respond to the tension by accepting an alliance with one of his parents. He may start crying, and one parent will draw him close. The other parent, frustrated, withdraws to the other room. In this way the outsider to the original threesome becomes the insider of the next.

This process defuses the original conflict and provides an escape valve from tension and anger. Just as important, **triangulation prevents any direct attempts by the primary parties to resolve their differences. Although all families create triadic patterns, these patterns will become more rigid when the family is facing a change or undergoing stress, and will be more flexible in periods of calm. Rigid triangles allow people to avoid facing the need to change or acknowledge their contribution to the problem. They also limit the options for finding solutions which allow for meaningful change.**

Triangles are likely to occur at several levels in the family and the business. In the Smiths' case, Rob and Kathy are relying on Dorothy as a go-between to ease the tensions of working together.

In another composite example, Joe and his son Mike are locked in a disagreement over marketing strategy for the family plumbing-supply company. Both Joe and Mike, whose relationship always has been stormy, see each other as unresponsive and shortsighted, and both feel hopeless about ever reaching an agreement. At home, Joe's wife works hard to smooth over conflict, listening to complaints from both men and trying to get each to back down. At work, the store's manager is the go-between, constantly adopting strategies to ease tension and conflict.

While Joe's wife and the store manager are trying to help, their behavior could eventually foster a crisis. **Their mediation keeps Joe and Mike from addressing their differences and deciding on a strategy. It also delays their reaching any kind of personal peace. Both of the go-betweens need to retire from their thankless role by** sending Joe and Mike back to each other to talk. They can encourage father and son to express themselves and offer help in that difficult task, but they must stop helping the two continue to avoid talking directly to each other.

Triangles also are common in families where one sibling is not employed in the family business. In these cases, the sibling's feeling that the father doesn't value his or her abilities or potential erupts in conflict with the sibling who is in the business. Again, this pattern prevents the true conflict from being resolved.

In other cases, unresolved conflict between two parents can be expressed as conflict with children. If two parents approaching retirement disagree about their new post-retirement roles or plans, they may deflect this conflict onto their children in a way that defers the issue.

For instance, parents may unconsciously behave in ways that discourage their children from being competent and assuming power, since that will hasten their retirement. The children's failures then become a new focal point for the parents, removing the burden of resolving with each other their own post-retirement plans. This pattern can easily foster conflict among the children, driving the most capable ones out of the business and leaving the underachiever or rebel to bear the brunt of the parental conflict. This pattern is one John and Dorothy Smith might well understand, given their difficulty in making retirement plans.

Another triangling opportunity arises in the presence of a key non-family executive. This mature, trusted professional can easily be thrust into a role as go-between for a father and son, a brother and sister, or other family members.

In-laws can easily be pulled into triangles. Uncomfortable with conflict in the workplace, some family members may take their troubles home with them and allow the spouse to carry the message. The problem thereby becomes a family issue, instead of a business issue, and the in-law may be assigned the blame as a troublemaker. "My daughter-in-law is so difficult. She's always complaining about the business," a parent may grumble, without realizing that the daughter-in-law is reflecting the feelings of his son. If the son feels underpaid, the daughter-in-law's complaints may lead to criticism that "she spends too much." If the son resents a sibling in the business, the daughter-in-law may be blamed for being "too critical."

Family members can turn triangles to advantage. (Please see Table 2.) A family member in the go-between role can use his or her influence with the other two triangle participants to stabilize and strengthen their relationships. When a son complains to his mother that his father is squelching his ideas at work, for instance, the mother's message might be: "Yes, I see that you're bothered by this. It seems to me that some changes in your working relationship with Dad need to be made. I know you're

TABLE 2

TURNING FAMILY TRIANGLES
TO HELPFUL TOOLS

*Some tips for family members
caught in the "go-between" role:*

- Don't keep secrets for others

- Focus on your own role in resolving the conflict, not on what you think others should do

- Encourage the other two participants to keep talking to each other

- Use statements beginning with "I"

- Ask questions that encourage others to use statements beginning with "I"

- Encourage constructive ways for the other participants to express themselves

strong enough to express that clearly to him and to hear his point of view."

This message supports and affirms the son and encourages him to resolve his problems directly with his father, without undermining the two men in any way. Similarly, the father might later complain to Mom, "I'm so frustrated with our son's inability to run his new division. Every time he comes in to talk, he has some hare-brained idea that has nothing to do with the operating problems over there." Mom might agree that such a situation is frustrating and that something needs to be done. She might also sympathize about the difficulties of turning over management authority to the next generation.

But instead of delivering any part of Dad's message to her son, she might suggest to her husband that the son could benefit from some thoughtful coaching from his father, and encourage Dad to approach the son with his concerns in a supportive way. This reminds the father of his appropriate role in relation to his son and encourages him to carry it out. In this way, Mom serves as a stabilizing, constructive force, helping the son and father resolve their problems directly.

In trying to act as peacemaker for Kathy and Rob, Dorothy Smith is unwittingly adhering to this most common of triangle patterns: "Mom-in-the-middle." In her well-meaning intervention, she is easing the tension just enough so that Kathy and Rob aren't forced to resolve their own problems. She may also unwittingly be distracting her and John's attention from their own difficult task of retirement planning by perpetuating the conflict between Rob and Kathy. If the kids aren't getting along, it's certainly no time to take off, John may reason. The net effect will only be to complicate the changes faced by the Smith clan.

As discussed, Dorothy can change her communications with Rob and Kathy in a way that strengthens their relationship, rather than worsening their conflict.

Differentiation of Self: The Core Concept

Unknown to each other, John's retirement announcement sets off in both John and Rob an internal struggle to define their responsibilities — to themselves, to each other and to the business.

John has always tried to give Rob a "lot of space," partly to compensate for the day-to-day closeness they experience in the family business. He doesn't want to interfere with his son's decisionmaking regarding the business and he doesn't want Rob to feel pressured. At the same time, John feels he has a right to retire and pass on the business to his children. A part of him feels Rob should be grateful. Yet he is disturbed at his son's apparent unhappiness.

For his part, Rob feels responsible for the future of the business, particularly since he will inherit part of it. As the oldest child and the only son in the Smith family, Rob also wants his father to have a peaceful retirement. Yet he feels increasingly overloaded and even resentful that his personal dreams seem to be fading. He finds it harder and harder to concentrate on the job.

■

The core of Bowen's systems approach to understanding how families work is the degree to which an individual can distinguish between the *feeling* process and the *intellectual* process. The feeling or emotional process includes states ranging from contentment and satisfaction to aggression, anger and sadness. The intellectual process includes the ability to think, reason and reflect, and enables people to govern their lives according to logic, intellect and reason.

A person who is "differentiated" is one who is highly able to

distinguish between feeling and thinking. **While the person can recognize, honor and express feelings when appropriate, he or she is able even under stress to recognize the difference between emotion and rational thought, to value all of those cues, and to react in a way that takes into account both the reality of the situation and the reality of his or her emotional response.** This enables one to adapt and be flexible even in times of extreme anxiety.

A differentiated person may be highly aware of others and may enjoy relationships with people who are similarly well differentiated, but he or she is not swallowed up by either feelings or rationality. He or she has plenty of energy left over for independent life goals.

People with the least differentiation of self, those who cannot distinguish between the feeling process and the intellectual process, are described as experiencing a high degree of *fusion*. **People whose emotions and intellect are fused may be trapped in either a feeling or a rational world. Those dominated by emotions may have great difficulty with the functioning of their lives. They may be totally oriented to their relationships, constantly seeking love and approval. Such people may be trapped within a feeling world.**

On the other hand, **poorly differentiated people may also be trapped within a rational world. People who cannot identify and express their feelings also have a high percentage of life's problems, including emotional illness, troublesome relationships and poor adjustment. Their feelings blocked, these people may become "overrational"** — unable to be flexible in responding to life's events or to deal with others in a way that takes into account their emotions.

This concept holds that all individuals fall at some point on a continuum between the extremes of high and low differentiation. Their progress along this spectrum strongly influences the degree to which they feel "out of control" or "in control" of their lives. As an individual achieves higher levels of differentiation, he or she can savor more fully the rewards of setting and achieving personal life goals, as well as enjoying the emotional closeness and comfort provided by the family. And in times of stress of the sort John and Rob Smith are experiencing, a person who normally feels "in control" may begin having trouble differentiating between emotion and intellect.

A related idea is that of "emotional maturity." In her book

> *A person who is "differentiated" is one who is highly able to distinguish between feeling and thinking.*

24

Reweaving the Family Tapestry: A Multigenerational Approach to Family (Norton & Co., New York, 1991), Fredda Herz defines emotional maturity as "the degree to which one is able to think and feel, to define oneself without emotionally reacting (to others' positions).... One who is emotionally mature is clear about boundaries between self and other and is aware when his or her actions are in reaction to the other."

Emotional maturity also describes the ability of a person to take responsibility for oneself in relation to others. Failure to take self-responsibility can take many forms, ranging from acquiescing to other people's needs to rebelling against other people's expectations. A person who is constantly helping others and making sure no one is hurt or upset, for instance, may be failing to take responsibility for herself and her own need for expressing opinions and ideas. On the other hand, a person who works until he drops and neglects personal relationships isn't taking responsibility for his own need for rest, recreation and emotional connection with others.

Both John and Rob Smith are experiencing some tension in this regard. Each is struggling to define his responsibilities to himself and to others. And each is struggling to deal with the strong feelings raised by this turning point in their lives. Rob is extremely responsible to himself and others in carrying out his duties at the business, but it is far more difficult for him to be true to himself in mapping out his life's work. His feelings of frustration and resentment are a signal that something is amiss in this area.

Levels of emotional maturity can be passed on from generation to generation. Family members can discover these patterns and turn them to their advantage by examining their own thoughts and feelings and determining how they are influencing their actions.

One step toward greater emotional maturity may be as simple as reminding oneself to stop and think before acting. A family member may feel enraged, for instance, that his brother continually criticizes him behind his back. His "natural" reaction may be to strike back by undermining one of his brother's projects. A more emotionally mature response: for the family member to recognize and honor his feelings of anger without being ruled by them, but rather by making a conscious decision about how to respond. If he truly takes responsibility for his actions, the family member may decide to

Emotional maturity describes the ability of a person to take responsibility for oneself in relation to others.

25

TABLE 3

STEPS TOWARD EMOTIONAL MATURITY

- Try in even the toughest situations to **stop and think**

- Take a hard, searching look at your own feelings about the problem situation

- Acknowledge your feelings honestly, honoring their importance

- Examine how your feelings are affecting your actions

- Examine your actions: Do they reflect the way you truly want to behave?

- Make a choice, without blaming others, about how **you** want to act in this situation.

break the cycle of destructive behavior and talk directly to his brother about the criticism.

In Rob Smith's case, a clear-headed recognition that his feelings are legitimate and significant — though they need not dominate his actions — could go far in helping him resolve his conflict over his future.

Family Structure: How Patterns Are Set.

Rob knew he should try to talk with his father about his role in the business, but he found it extraordinarily difficult. He could not remember a time since childhood when he and his father had discussed their hopes and dreams. He and John often talked for hours about the business, sharing the smallest details about new products or processes. These subjects were tacitly viewed as "men's issues" within the Smith family, and Rob knew Kathy often wished she was part of the discussions.

Yet Rob also knew that while women in the family were usually excluded from those talks, Dorothy and Kathy were the ones John turned to with his heartfelt hopes and goals. Thus Rob wasn't surprised to learn that John had discussed his retirement plans with Kathy at length before announcing them, while Rob knew nothing about them at all.

■

Another dimension of the family system — family structure — helps determine the ways family members talk and relate to one another. Essentially, family structure is the way in which family patterns of relating are organized. These patterns reflect the degree to which individual family members are emotionally connected to one another. Together, they comprise a kind of "social network" that orders family relationships.

As defined by family systems theorist Salvadore Minuchin in his book, *Families and Family Therapy* (Harvard University Press, 1974), family structure is "the invisible fit of functional demands that organizes the ways in which family members interact. Repeated transactions establish patterns of how, when and to whom to relate, and these patterns underpin the system."

While this concept seems abstract, family structure has a major day-to-day impact on how families work together and solve problems. As in the Smith family, a father might only talk to his sons about business, and only to his daughters about emotional matters. The mother might be listened to by others on issues of personal health or conduct, but her advice on careers or business issues might be disregarded. Children, regardless of their age, might be shielded from discussions about their parents' health.

This results in different decisionmaking patterns around different family themes. The mother and father might have long discussions about health worries, but they might brush off their children's questions on the same subject. "You don't need to worry about that," the parents might say, even though their health is obviously a major concern to their children.

If the family structure becomes too rigid, individuals may feel confined, frustrated or rebellious. In times of stress, the family structure may hamper important communications, as is happening with John and Rob Smith. One remedy: for an individual family member to develop as many authentic, one-to-one relationships with other family members as possible. These relationships can serve as a bridge enabling individuals to transcend family patterns of communication and decisionmaking and to accomplish needed change.

Develop as many authentic, one-to-one relationships with other family members as possible.

How Boundaries Affect Family Closeness

As John's retirement approaches, Dorothy feels increasingly anxious. She loses interest in the volunteer work that has engaged her in the past and finds herself worrying to an uncomfortable degree about Rob and Kathy. She absorbs herself in listening to her children's complaints about each other's work and intervening to try to make peace when she can. She finds herself staying around the house more, and thinking about plans for family activities. And she worries about how the family will stay close after John retires from the business, which has been "the linchpin of the Smith family" for decades, in John's words.

Dorothy also finds herself reminiscing about the early days of the business, when she and John worked side by side at the office, and about the years when Rob and Kathy were young. But when she tries to imagine herself and John enjoying retirement, the images in her mind soon dissolve and she begins to feel anxious. While John has tried to bring up retirement, she changes the subject. The idea of making serious plans just makes her more uneasy.

■

A part of each family's internal structure or organization is a system of boundaries — the invisible barriers that determine family members' emotional distance from each other and from the outside world.

Families display varying degrees of cohesiveness, as detailed in Minuchin's research. **Some families become so attached and dependent at an emotional level, or "enmeshed," that they lose a sense of individual boundaries**. In these families, boundaries between individuals tend to be more permeable and less rigid, while boundaries between the family and the outside world are less flexible and more rigid. (See Figure 2.)

Members of enmeshed families rely on each other for a wide range of needs. In enmeshed families, each individual's activities tend to be known and discussed by other members. Everyone seeks advice from other family members, particularly on important life decisions. Keeping something private is seen as a hostile, withholding act.

In contrast, **disengaged families sanction independence, privacy and individualism. Members share little information about each other and they avoid interfering in each other's thoughts, decisions or actions.** In these families, boundaries between individuals tend to be more clearly drawn, while boundaries between the family and the outside world are less rigid. (See Figure 2.) Members may have different friends and work at different places. They may be able to have fun with or get advice from people outside the immediate family more readily than

FIGURE 2

Boundaries in Enmeshed and Disengaged Families

THE ENMESHED FAMILY

THE DISENGAGED FAMILY

members of enmeshed families. The level of emotion is low in disengaged families, while it can be extremely high in enmeshed families.

Neither an enmeshed nor disengaged style of family interaction is "healthy" or "unhealthy." Only at the extremes is either enmeshment or disengagement viewed as unhealthy; most families fall between the two extremes. A family that is too enmeshed may discourage individual members' autonomous exploration and mastery of new skills. An extremely disengaged family, in contrast, may develop members who have a strong sense of independence but lack a capacity for interdependence and for asking for support when they need it.

As Dorothy is discovering, many families go through both enmeshed and disengaged cycles, depending upon children's ages or the parents' stages in life. Families with very young children may be more enmeshed, for instance, and move toward greater disengagement as the children grow up. Sometimes, family members in business together find themselves interacting and relying upon each other more, simply because their lives at work and home overlap in so many ways. This can tend to place business families toward the "enmeshed" end of the spectrum.

Under stress, some family members may move toward one extreme or another. In Dorothy's case, she is yearning for the family's return to a more enmeshed state, reflecting her anxiety about John's leaving the business and their retirement. As is often true, Dorothy's strong feelings about family closeness are a signal that the issue needs some attention.

Family Roles, Formal and Informal. Within each family, individuals play a rich variety of roles in relation to each other. These roles may be formal ones, determined by the family member's birth order or relationships to siblings, parents or spouses. Or they may be informal, relating to a particular style or way of behaving that the individual has carved out for himself or herself within the family.

Either way, these roles — parental roles, child roles, spousal roles, gender roles, sibling and other roles, including informal ones — can have a powerful impact on the workings of a family, particularly if members are unconscious of them. One of the best reasons for examining and acknowledging these roles is to make sure that they allow individuals the flexibility to change as needed. The gender roles

Many families go through both enmeshed and disengaged cycles, depending upon children's ages or the parents' stages in life.

30

TABLE 4

RECOGNIZING YOUR FAMILY'S RELATIONSHIP STYLE

Families that are enmeshed tend to:

- Foster a sense of loyalty and belonging
- Encourage interdependence
- Cultivate empathy
- Have the same interests
- Spend most of their time together
- Speak for each other
- Interrupt each other
- Explain each other's feelings
- Assume members understand each other
- Discourage autonomous exploration

Families that are disengaged tend to:

- Tolerate differences
- Foster a sense of personal independence
- Respect separate views
- Cultivate self-reliance
- Spend little time together
- Disregard each other's feelings or wishes
- Block communications on certain subjects
- Avoid close contact
- Lack empathetic responses
- Fail to listen to or hear each other

unconsciously adhered to in the Smith family, for instance, where men seldom engage in talk of hopes and dreams and women are excluded from nuts-and-bolts business discussions, are inhibiting John and Rob from addressing some major issues that are affecting them.

Also, awareness of roles can avert potential conflict. Ellen M. Perry, executive vice president of Asset Management Advisors Inc., warns family business owners against exercising their parental role in too rigid a fashion. Forbidding mature children from sharing certain business information with their spouses can create distrust in marriages, Perry says. It also can force the child to take sides between his or her parents and spouse, or reinforce the in-law's feelings of being an outsider.

Let's take a closer look at a few examples of the kinds of family roles that affect family businesses.

Birth Order: The Family Constellation

As the months wear on toward John Smith's planned retirement, Rob feels an increasing burden of responsibility. As the oldest child, Rob feels the need to act as standard-bearer for the family. He has always felt a sense of responsibility for Kathy and for the welfare of the family as a whole. As John Smith begins to step back from day-to-day operations of the business, Rob feels he must fill the gap, taking charge and controlling events at the office. Unconsciously, he feels that in the eyes of his parents, failing to do so would disappoint them and violate his special role.

■

Sibling relationships are a special subsystem of the family system, in which patterns set in motion during childhood tend to persist. A family systems approach holds that people born in the same sibling position tend to have common characteristics. Within families, the differences between children born at different points in the birth order can prove a rich vein of diversity and talent.

The pioneering work of clinical psychologist Walter Toman suggests that **firstborn children** tend to be seen as special, receive a great deal of attention, and often are trained to take on responsibility and a leadership role. Oldest children tend to care for and protect the siblings that follow.

Youngest children are also special because they are last. They are usually in the company of others, so they grow up seeking to be understood by others. They tend to focus inward, rather than on the outside world. They may have more freedom to experiment because other siblings were caring for family responsibilities. And although they are competitive, they know how to give in to someone older and more powerful.

Middle children often have a hard time getting noticed. They tend to look outside the family for recognition or satisfaction, or to learn how to exert a lot of pressure within the family to get attention. Because the middle child has to vie with two special siblings on either end of the birth order, he or she often becomes skilled in negotiating for resources and attention.

Only children are very special in the family. They often seek the attention of authority figures, since they are accustomed to interacting with adults. They may grow up with less experience at having to share limited resources or solve problems with siblings. Though they may cultivate a sense of self-sufficiency, they have less opportunity to cooperate and collaborate with others.

In the family business, only children may also grow up feeling they have less choice about their role in the business, with no siblings to share responsibility for the next generation of management.

The same-sex parent can have a big impact on birth order roles because she or he serves as a model for many of the same qualities affected by birth order. If, as in Rob Smith's case, the oldest child is a son and the father was also an oldest child, the qualities common to oldest children are reinforced. Conversely, if the parent occupied a different slot in the birth order, the traits are moderated.

Birth order can be an asset to a family business, fostering the rich variety of personality traits and types needed to run a company. The first-born, for instance, may contribute strong leadership skills. The middle child may bring to the business a gift for constructive negotiation. And the youngest child may be a talented innovator.

In the Willard family hardware-distribution firm, birth order helped create an effective second-generation management team. Al, the first-born, was a serious child who often baby-sat for his younger brother, Hank, and helped him with his homework. Conscientious and consistent, Al was voted "Most Likely to Succeed" in his high school graduating class and went on to earn respectable grades as an accounting major at the state university.

Hank, on the other hand, was always the family troublemaker. Charming and impulsive, he delighted in practical jokes and sometimes cut classes. But he excelled under pressure and sometimes showed flashes of brilliance, winning rave reviews in lead roles in his class plays and going on to major in speech at a small East Coast college.

When the Willard boys joined the family business — Al straight out of college, and Hank after two years in sales for a big manufacturing concern — other family members shook their heads. "Those two will never get along as managers," an uncle predicted. "They are so different from each other."

Birth order can be an asset to a family business, fostering the variety of personality types needed to run a company.

But much to their relatives' surprise, Al and Hank developed a dynamic working relationship. Al delighted in managing Willard Co.'s finances, setting up accounting and data-processing systems. Hank, meanwhile, opened up a new sales territory and proceeded to put the Midwestern company on the map west of the Mississippi.

How do the boys get along behind the scenes? Great, they agree. "My brother is the one who talks to the board. He's good at that, and charming," says Al. "I figure out the proformas and he presents them. He can sell anything."

Hank adds, "I could never do the systems work that Al is so good at, and that makes the company hum. But I'm happy to take the show on the road once he's put it together!" Conscious of the power of teamwork, the two have turned their differences into a major asset.

In Rob Smith's case, birth order is affecting his attitudes toward the business and the family. Partly because he is the oldest son, Rob feels the burden of family responsibility so heavily that there seems to be no room to discuss his wishes for personal and career growth. If he felt free to place more importance on his personal wishes and desires, another path might be charted for Rob in the business that would allow him greater freedom to lead and come up with new ideas. Or he might find a way to discuss with his father his dream of starting his own practice. Instead, Rob's perception of his role in the Smith family system tells him he must simply comply with his father's implied expectations to share management control and run the business the same way John always has.

Sibling Rivalry: Healthy Tension Gone Awry

Kathy's plans for aggressive growth at Smith Printing increasingly irritate Rob. While Rob appreciates the innovations Kathy has achieved so far, he is worried about becoming too aggressive too soon after John's retirement. In the past, Kathy has followed Rob's advice on financial matters, which she knows aren't her forte. But now, when Rob brings up his concerns about the company's projected debt level, Kathy argues that risk-taking is necessary at this stage. At the same time, Rob notices, Kathy is spending far less time at home with Ken, her husband of two years, and she has stopped talking altogether about having children.

■

Most siblings experience some rivalry, and conflict is just as normal as cooperation in these relationships. Ideally, siblings both attach to and compete with each other, maintaining a healthy balance that encourages personal growth. If siblings learn during childhood to respect and accept each other's rights and differences, they can help each other prepare for adulthood. And if as adults they relate to each other as autonomous persons and are treated fairly by their parents, with respect shown for their individual differences, sibling relationships can foster creative collaboration.

Just as birth order can be a positive force in the family business, sibling rivalry can fuel energetic pursuit of both personal and business goals. When Harry Bronson, founder of a metals-fastener manufacturer, assigned each of his two children in the business a new sales territory, he was concerned about the effects of nose-to-nose rivalry. To his delight, he found his children seemed stimulated by the challenge. Not only did they work hard, but they engaged in an ongoing repartee at the office, kidding each other good-naturedly about minor foul-ups and foibles. The men even posted phony "sales charts" on their office walls, with each brother's chart showing his sibling's results plunging while his own sales soared. The friendly competition trickled down through the ranks, fostering gains in morale and productivity.

Sibling rivalry can intensify to destructive levels, however, when children compete for their parents' love and attention. Children who feel that they are loved for who they are have little need to attack or destroy their siblings to get attention. The opposite is true of those who are neglected or belittled. The pattern may intensify in family firms, because children often remain subordinate to their parents — and may feel locked into birth order positions — later in life than most children.

Parents set this process in motion by the ways in which they compare their children to each other, mete out resources (including parental love and attention) and resolve conflict, as discussed by Stewart D. Friedman in the *Family Business Review* ("Sibling Relationships and Intergenerational Succession in Family Firms," Jossey-Bass Inc., Spring, 1991). If parents compare their offspring in ways that value each as unique individuals, but do not rigidly classify or stereotype them, the children are more likely to value themselves as individuals — and less likely to engage in prolonged, destructive sibling rivalry. Parents must allocate attention fairly among children, in a way that is *equitable* and not just *equal*. They should take into account individual differences without seeming to prefer one child over

Sibling rivalry can intensify to destructive levels when children compete for their parents' love and attention.

TABLE 5

SOWING THE SEEDS
OF SIBLING RIVALRY

Some ways parents help create rivalrous siblings:

- Comparing siblings in a way that classifies, stereotypes or otherwise diminishes one or the other.

- Allocating parental love and attention in a way that ignores individual differences.

- Interfering in siblings' efforts to resolve conflicts with each other.

— Stewart D. Friedman

another — a delicate balancing act, at best. Parents also need to avoid intruding on siblings' efforts to resolve conflicts, at risk of prolonging and reinforcing the rivalry.

Families can deal with destructive sibling rivalry in several ways, including talking privately with the brothers and sisters involved or encouraging them to attend family-business forums or seminars on conflict resolution or effective communications. Sometimes, if just one of the warring parties recognizes and decides to end unhealthy rivalry, he or she can accomplish that change by simply changing his or her own attitudes and behavior. A behavioral change by one person can have a transformative effect. (See Table 6.)

Ned and Lou Henson, both vice presidents of the family food-service business, never got along as children, and their relationship hasn't improved with age. Because their areas of responsibility — sales and distribution — overlap so broadly, they have to confer frequently. But each time they try to resolve a problem together, their conversation usually erupts into an argument. Problems begin cropping up in what should be routine transactions, and both men begin to dread going to work.

After talking with his wife about the problem and doing some soul-searching, Lou begins to see a pattern in his arguments with Ned, and he decides to try to change them. Instead of becoming angry when Ned accuses him of carelessness or ineptitude and firing off his own counter-charge about Ned's alleged perfectionism or slavish attention to detail, Lou decides to stay calm and simply ask Ned for more information about

TABLE 6

CHANGING NEGATIVE BEHAVIOR PATTERNS

Step One: One participant in the negative pattern sees, or is helped to see, its destructive impact.

Step Two: He or she begins to act differently, communicating a personal perspective without attacking.

Step Three: The other participant in the pattern responds with anxiety, sometimes redoubling accusations or other negative behavior.

Step Four: The first participant maintains his or her new, self-responsible position, remaining calmly supportive, but not accepting the invitation to take responsibility for taking over the other's pain.

the matter at hand. If he keeps his mind and conversation focused on the business issue, he reasons, he and Ned might have a better chance of solving some of their mutual problems.

The first time Lou tries his new approach, Ned seems taken aback. "You really fouled up this new order," Ned says. "How do you expect me to start weekly deliveries to this many new customers so soon?"

Ordinarily, Lou would respond with anger, accusing Ned of failing to appreciate the difficulty of bringing in new business or of having a "bean-counter" mentality. Instead, he says, "You say I fouled up the order. What did I do wrong? Is the problem the weekly schedule? Or do you need more time to get ready?"

Ned starts to shout a response, then falls silent for a moment before continuing a string of angry criticisms. When he finishes, Lou repeats a summary of Ned's points and agrees immediately to change some aspects of the order. He adds that he appreciates the pressure on Ned's department caused by a rush of new orders, but that in his experience, little can be done to space them out more regularly.

Though Lou's new approach enables the brothers to begin solving a few problems at work, Ned feels uneasy and frustrated. He has always been thrown off by surprises and worries about his inability to respond to the new orders effectively. When Lou's wife invites the family to their home for a traditional family Thanksgiving dinner, Ned refuses.

Lou is initially angry and is tempted to abandon his attempts at smoother relations. He tells his wife he feels vulnerable and betrayed. "What's the point of putting in all this effort if Ned is just going to act *worse*?" he wonders aloud. "I'm not surprised that he's having a hard time," Lou's wife comments. "He has to have everything in his life in order...your family always teases him about that." Her remark makes Lou realize that Ned's reaction may not be entirely a criticism of him. Rather, it may be a reflection of Ned's anxiety. With that support, he stays the course, being more careful to give Ned advance warning of potential new orders. Gradually, the brothers' relationship begins to take a lasting turn for the better.

This example affirms two important principles for families working together in business. First, one person can accomplish change — not by trying to manipulate or control others, but by simply changing himself or herself. And second, changing patterns of family relationships may cause a temporary *increase* in anxiety and disquiet in the family before the change is complete.

Informal Family Roles. Beyond formal roles related to gender, marital status or parent-child or sibling relationships, some family members assume informal roles based on personality or other factors. A common one is that of the "black sheep," the member who defies family standards of conduct or decisionmaking in favor of rebellion. The court jester, the mediator, the achiever, the troublemaker, the apologist, the spectator, the taskmaster, the socialist, the religious person — all may be roles in the family context that influence individual members' behavior.

Like other roles within the family, these informal roles often arise from the dynamics of the family as a whole. Every troublemaker may be balanced by an overachiever, and every black sheep by a do-gooder. The roles should be taken lightly and should not be permitted to confine individual family members to certain ways of behaving.

Nevertheless, understanding informal roles can be useful in two ways. First, it can help the roleplayer maintain a sense of personal identity separate from his or her family role. The black sheep, for

One person can accomplish change — not by trying to manipulate or control others, but by simply changing himself or herself.

38

instance, may point out at a family meeting that the family's favorite charity has been neglecting some of the goals most prized by the family. "Oh, there goes the black sheep, criticizing family decisions again," other members may respond. But if the family is conscious of the power of these informal roles and has put them in their proper perspective, members will be able to separate the merit of the comment from the attributes of the role. The "black sheep" is then free to reply, with justification and a smile, "Yes, but this time I'm right!"

Second, **examining these informal roles can sometimes encourage family members to shed old patterns and try new ones. The spectator may become more active, the comedian more serious, the responsible one more whimsical. The result: less predictability in family relations and, potentially, greater group effectiveness and creativity in decisionmaking.**

Emotional Cutoff: Denying the Ties That Bind

As Rob struggles with his father's expectations of him, he feels increasing anxiety. He yearns for an opportunity to strike out on his own, to prove that he can create something new. But he can find no opening to discuss this inner conflict with his father.

Out of concern for Rob, a couple of close friends urge him to consider leaving the family business before it's too late. As he wrestles in silence with the issue, Rob finds himself wondering about his father's early years. He remembers his mother mentioning a few times that John had left the family farm at 18 and become estranged from his father Frank Jr., who died when Rob was only seven. But Rob knows little about his grandfather, except that he had been a successful farmer in the Midwest who had passed on the farm to John's brother Michael shortly after John had left home.

■

All people are attached to their parents as children, and they separate from them in a variety of ways. In some cases, the bond loosens in a healthy, conscious way as children gradually gain self-sufficiency with the support and guidance of parents. In others, people sever the

Changing patterns of family relationships may cause a temporary increase in anxiety and disquiet in the family before the change is complete.

39

ties abruptly by isolating themselves, withdrawing or running away. This doesn't resolve the child's need to go through a detachment process, and it also denies the importance of the parental family. This phenomenon is called emotional cutoff. The way an individual handles the process can resonate through the generations.

While American society often misunderstands emotional cutoff as "growing up," or as a necessary step toward independence, it is in fact just the opposite. **The person who runs away emotionally from his family of origin is as dependent as the one who never leaves home.** The more intense the cutoff with the past, the more likely the person is to experience the same family problems in his or her own adult partnerships as existed in the parental home.

Sometimes, the cutoff of a family member can be a symptom of a larger family problem. In such cases, one individual becomes a target or focal point for all the tension arising from the problem. The person may in some way have broken the family's or society's rules, but he or she is not solely responsible for the family's emotional circumstances. Rather, the individual becomes a receptacle for the uneasiness and anxiety that all members feel and unwittingly acts out their negative feelings.

In the example above, Rob Smith has been placed in a position of isolation within the family. His father, himself conflicted about retiring, has planned Rob's future without consulting Rob. Kathy is engrossed in her own plans for the business. Dorothy is unwittingly making things harder for Rob by perpetuating his conflict with Kathy. Thus Rob is on a kind of desert island already. In some ways, he has become a receptacle for the family's anxieties and fears about succession.

Though Rob is not eager to take his friends' advice and abandon the family business, this potentiality is more real than it might seem. As discussed below, the Smith family is unwittingly recreating a pattern of behavior rooted in its past, raising the possibility that Rob may be cut off from the family.

Genograms As A Tool for Understanding

"The past is the present. It's the future too."
— Eugene O'Neill
Long Day's Journey Into Night

■

The idea that family patterns perpetuate themselves through the generations raises issues that can seem unfathomable. How can one identify

TABLE 7

GLOSSARY OF FAMILY SYSTEMS TERMS**

Differentiation: The ability of an individual to distinguish between emotional and intellectual functioning. In relationships, the ability to maintain a solid, non-negotiable self and to take comfortable "I" positions. A primary yardstick of psychological health, according to Bowen's family systems theory. The differentiated person can risk genuine emotional closeness without undue anxiety.

Fusion: The quality of blending emotions and intellect so that one is unable to distinguish between the two. The degree to which mutually interconnection relationships are "stuck together." In fused relationships, none of the individuals can move independently of the others or the whole.

Enmeshment: An intense level of emotional closeness in families. The quality of being so interdependent emotionally that individuals' boundaries crumble and personal privacy is nonexistent.

Disengagement: A low level of emotional closeness in families. The quality of being so independent emotionally that individuals avoid supporting each other or sharing in each other's thoughts, decisions or actions.

Triangling: The process of bringing a third person into a two-person relationship in order to defuse the tension within the original dyad. Prevents direct resolution of conflict by the twosome.

Birth order: The tendency of one's position in the sequence of a family's childbirths to affect the roles and perceptions that the person carries through life. Other things being equal, persons who occupy the same relative position among their family's children will share common characteristics.

Sibling rivalry: A conflictual tendency that begins when children compete at a young age for their parents' love and attention, and can continue through the children's adult lives in the family business. While a certain amount of sibling rivalry can foster creativity and growth, it has a damaging impact if taken to extremes.

Emotional cutoff: Isolating oneself, withdrawing or running away from one's unresolved emotional attachments to parents in an effort to restart life in a new generation. While the cutoff process may feel like a declaration of independence, it in fact merely submerges unresolved emotional attachment to the parental family and leaves the individual as emotionally dependent as the one who never leaves home.

**SOURCE: Dr. Murray Bowen, Ph.D.

one's own family characteristics and patterns and trace them through the generations?

An exercise that has helped many families is to create a genogram. **A genogram is an information-rich format for drawing a family tree.** It records data about family members and their relationships over at least three generations, as described by Monica McGoldrick and Randy Gerson in *Genograms in Family Assessment* (W.W. Norton & Co., 1985), a source for much of the description that follows.

A genogram shows names and ages of family members; dates of birth, marriage, separation, divorce, death and so on; and dated notations about occupations, significant life events, residences, illnesses, changes in life plans and other major events in the family's history. It also shows the nature of key relationships, portraying them as close, conflictual, fused, distant and so on.

A genogram is a uniquely useful tool to help a family see the intergenerational patterns of life events and behaviors that are affecting them today. The process of preparing one can encourage family members to look at family issues in new ways. Once complete, the genogram may be used by family members, as well as historians, therapists, family business consultants and others, to analyze or convey a great deal of family information.

It is important to note that **a genogram is not a predictor of family behavior. It suggests tendencies, not ironclad behavioral rules.** It is only a tool for forming hypotheses about family functioning — hunches that serve as a starting point for further exploration.

Nevertheless, through its use of schematics, the genogram often shows better than the proverbial "thousand words" how a family history, with its rich patterns of family events, values and ways of interrelating, is still alive in the present and influencing family members. Because family members are depicted graphically by lines on the genogram, it is easier to see how their behavior is interrelated and how these patterns affect individuals.

A genogram is a uniquely useful tool to help a family see the intergenerational patterns of life events and behaviors that are affecting them today.

EXHIBIT 1

Key to Symbols Used in a Genogram

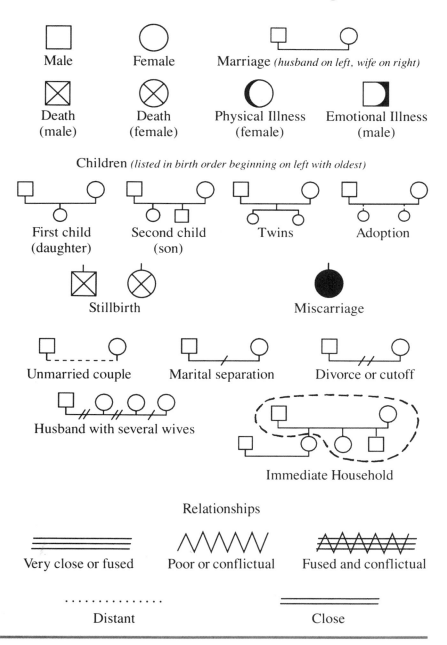

Male Female Marriage *(husband on left, wife on right)*

Death (male) Death (female) Physical Illness (female) Emotional Illness (male)

Children *(listed in birth order beginning on left with oldest)*

First child (daughter) Second child (son) Twins Adoption

Stillbirth Miscarriage

Unmarried couple Marital separation Divorce or cutoff

Husband with several wives Immediate Household

Relationships

Very close or fused Poor or conflictual Fused and conflictual

Distant Close

VI. *Unlocking the Barriers to the Past*

As the year leading up to John Smith's planned retirement wears on, he prepares to work with a family-business consultant on the financial issues raised by ownership succession. But he is hampered by a growing sense that all the fun seems to have drained out of life. Rob and Kathy are avoiding one another, and they argue a lot when they do work together. Though some major decisions loom, no one is sitting down to talk about them — strategic planning, for instance.

Worse yet, Rob has grown more distant and stopped coming to some family gatherings, plunging Dorothy into a bout of intense worry. John worries that Dorothy is losing interest in the volunteer activities that so engaged her just a year ago, and she refuses to talk about retirement plans. John's concerns about his children's ability to manage the business are mounting so fast that he fears he may have to postpone retirement anyway.

In private moments, John sometimes wonders how a simple decision to retire could breed such a thicket of family problems. He wonders if he made a mistake announcing his retirement at the family meeting. He begins increasing his hours at the office again, and loyal co-workers are startled to see him do something he has never done before: close his office door. As he mulls things over, he tells himself, "I need to try to understand what everybody is going through here." He resolves to ask some questions about how other family members are feeling.

In his first session with the family business consultant, John lays out some of his concerns. As he talks, he begins to realize the magnitude of the changes he is undertaking:

He is trying to prepare a new generation for leadership. He is trying to let go of the business that had been his life, as well as the glue that held the Smith family together. He is contemplating new terms for his life together with his wife. He is restructuring his financial future as he plans for retirement. And he is trying to pass on a lifetime's assets to his children.

"No wonder you feel overwhelmed," the consultant observed. "You are facing not one, but many major changes in your life and your business, all at once. And you've only given yourself a year to accomplish all these things."

Just naming the stresses helped John feel better. Not only does the consultant encourage John to seek out other family members for talks, but he urges him to lead the family in an expanded continuity-planning effort, including a group activity he had never even considered: a close look, via a genogram, at the workings of the Smith family, ranging from its special attributes and values to its history.

■

The consultant suggests constructing a diagram for the Smiths for two reasons. First, several confusing behaviors are surfacing among family members at once, suggesting that a look at family patterns might be enlightening. Second, at a time when communication has become difficult, the process of preparing a genogram can act as a catalyst for the family to rediscover its most deeply felt connections and loyalties. At John's suggestion, the family begins a series of family meetings aimed not only at smoothing succession, but at understanding better the workings of the family.

The genogram can be helpful in several respects, the consultant explains. First, it shows patterns of *household structure*, including household composition. Does the family have a history of intact nuclear-family households? Divorce and remarriage? Three-generational households? Patterns such as these could provide a starting point for understanding current family members' feelings and tendencies around these issues. Sibling patterns, including gender and the timing of a child's birth in the family's history, are also important. Was the patriarch the oldest child of an oldest child? This could explain the high expectations and sense of specialness he assigns to his own oldest son. Was one child born after a series of miscarriages? That might result in the child's growing up with a feeling of being special. If an older child was born before the miscarriages, he or she might have had to cope with a sense that parents were unavailable during that time of sadness and loss.

Second, the genogram shows *life cycle* patterns, including how a family progresses through such milestones as leaving home, marriage, the birth of children, retirement and so on. Have most members of the family married young, retired late or had their children in their 20s? The fact that three sons in a family married for the first time in their 50s, for instance, might indicate some problems in leaving home and forming intimate relationships.

Third, the genogram shows *pattern repetition across generations*. Recognizing repetitive patterns of behavior — such as a tendency to strong sibling teamwork, strong marital partnerships, extreme success or failure on the part of different siblings in the same family, or difficulties with alcoholism or divorce — can help family members of the present generation understand and appreciate such tendencies and use that knowledge to make conscious, informed choices and to live more fully.

Fourth, the genogram shows how *life events affect family functioning*. Seemingly unconnected events such as deaths, broken engagements and marriages can affect a family's functioning in unconscious ways. Families are more vulnerable to change or disruption during major reorganizations or transitions. The untimely death or suicide of a parent, for instance, may trigger divorce, drug abuse or emotional upheaval. In some families, certain events take on special significance because of what has happened in the past.

Fifth, the genogram shows *relational patterns and triangles* that can repeat themselves through generations. Close father-son or mother-daughter relationships can crop up repeatedly as a source of family strength, for instance. Triangles involving a mother and two siblings can produce adults who tend to function in the same way with their own children. These relationship characteristics can be shown on the genogram so that members of the present generation can see how their family relations reflect the whole system.

Finally, genograms reflect the degree of *family balance and imbalance*. This is a more abstract idea; basically, it shows how the position of one member in the family system affects the position of others. If an oldest child is a responsible, "take-charge" sort of person, the younger may be freer to experiment and explore new lifestyles. If the oldest child tends to be a caretaker, the youngest may tend to find relationships in which he or she is taken care of by others. This can affect marriages: An oldest child and youngest child who marry each other may find a harmonious balance of expectations. On the other hand, if two youngest children marry each other, each may be looking for the other to care for him or her, creating an imbalance and perhaps tension or conflict.

A family of high achievers may find balance by tolerating periods of low achievement by each individual member at various stages of life; on the other hand, the family may have just one member who does poorly all the time, suggesting that the low achiever may singlehandedly be providing some "balance" to the family system. In some marriages, spouses alternate in supporting each other during periods of stress or need. In alcoholic marriages, however, one spouse may consistently play a complementary role to the alcoholic, acting as the overresponsible partner to balance the alcoholic's failure to assume responsibility. While some balances can be healthy and normal, others push the compensating family member into positions of self-sacrifice or overload that he or she can't or doesn't want to maintain for long.

EXHIBIT 2

The Smith Family Genogram
1990 – The Year of John's Retirement

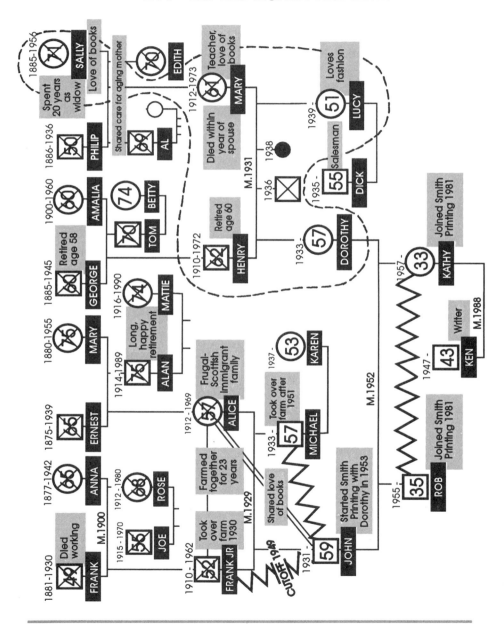

A Confluence of Strengths — and Stresses. Using the genogram as a discussion tool, the Smiths discover, some remarkable strengths and models of success in the family's past. For instance:

- The family has a history of strong nuclear families, with high value placed on children and family closeness.

- They share a love for books and high-quality printed literature, as manifested by the business.

- Family members share a strong legacy of spousal teamwork, with women making a major contribution to family enterprises.

- The Smiths have a legacy of sibling teamwork.

- The family has a noteworthy ability to pull together in times of intense stress.

- Among the Smith forebears are some who have enjoyed unusually long, happy retirements.

- John and Rob share a strong sense of adventure, as well as some of the role expectations conferred by their birth-order positions as firstborns.

These insights re-energize family members and as a result, they feel better able to tackle the challenges of succession.

At the same time, the Smiths learn much about the stresses they are experiencing. In brief:

- John is reaching a stage in life that caused significant conflict and cutoff in his own family of origin.

- Dorothy is approaching a life phase that creates a great deal of anxiety for her about health, longevity and family closeness.

- Rob at 35 is passing through a life stage that for his father resulted in a cutoff from his own father. He is facing what he feels may be his last significant opportunity to restructure his life's work in a way that is more satisfying to him. Yet as the oldest son of an oldest son of an oldest son, he is torn by a strong sense of responsibility to the family and the business.

> *As the oldest son of an oldest son of an oldest son, he is torn by a strong sense of responsibility to the family and the business.*

■ Kathy and Rob are wrestling with problems of a kind that have caused sibling conflict in the Smith family in the past.

■ And Kathy, at 33 and two years into her marriage to a man 10 years her senior, is well into her peak years for child-bearing — just as her father's retirement poses an unprecedented business opportunity in her life.

A Cautionary Note. As the Smith family begins its discussions, the consultant points out that any observations based on the genogram are only hypotheses. **Predictions based on genograms are not fact. They should be used only as clues to guide the family's further explorations into new ways of functioning.** Ideally, the consultant says, the genogram will continue to serve as a departure point for the Smiths to develop a deeper understanding of the workings of their family and the emotions and events they are experiencing.

Family Values: Adventure and Entrepreneurship. As the Smiths examine their genogram and discuss the lives of their forebears, a pattern of adventurousness emerges. Against the wishes of his immigrant parents in Philadelphia, John's grandfather Frank ventured west as a young man to Indiana, where he bought a chunk of rich, cheap farmland and settled down with Anna, an energetic, careful woman from a farm family with a strong attachment to the land. Frank's son Frank Jr. had few choices about his life's work; he took over the farm at 20, after his father died unexpectedly of a heart attack while working in the fields.

But Frank's grandson John would experience a similar restlessness and sense of adventure when, at 18, he left the farm to attend college and start his own business in the city. With no financial help from his parents and little to guide him but a love of books and machinery, he started Smith Printing from scratch.

As the family talks, Rob looks at his father with a new appreciation. Just like Rob, John felt a need as a young man to start something new, that was uniquely his own. Rob resolves to try to talk with his father about his own restlessness.

The Smith Roots: A Love for Books and Printing. The Smiths have always been proud of their products — high-quality printed materials and collectible books — and enjoyed holding and enjoying a finely bound printed work. But as they get better acquainted with their ancestors, they recognize that their appreciation is a multigenerational passion. Dorothy's mother Mary was a teacher who loved teaching reading and volunteered in the public library. Dorothy's grandmother Sally, who lived with Dorothy's family for a time, treasured books and taught her grandchildren to handle the works in her library with care and respect. As Dorothy reminisces, she describes the way Sally touched her rare volumes, as though they were fine china or gems, and pointed out to the children the quality of the materials and the look and feel of the binding. Dorothy wonders aloud if her own choice of a literature major during her two years of college arose partly from that legacy.

Similarly, John's mother passed on to her son a love for reading. As the family discusses the pattern, Kathy and her husband Ken smile. A writer of children's books, Ken never realized that his vocation might have been part of his appeal to Kathy. Kathy points out the link to the others, eliciting laughter, and John jokes, "Let's just hope you carry on the legacy by reading your own books to our grandchildren!"

A Legacy of Sibling and Spousal Teamwork. The Smiths also discover a pattern of family members' pulling together when times get tough. When Dorothy's grandmother, a widow, became too frail to live by herself, Dorothy's mother Mary and her two brothers and one sister took turns caring for her in their homes. The resulting burden was not too heavy on any of the families involved, and all the grandchildren benefited from getting to know Sally well before she died.

Similarly, after John's grandfather died abruptly at the depths of the Great Depression, Frank Jr. and his wife Alice, the frugal daughter of Scottish immigrants, threw themselves into a lifelong struggle to keep the farm afloat. Not only did they work side by side in the fields, but Alice kept the books, managing money so well that the family avoided the debt that sank so many family farms of that era.

As the story unfolds, John reminisces about how he and his brother worked hard together on his father's farm for several years. Though some tensions arose between them just before John left, their relations for the most part had been good. Rob's and Kathy's eyes meet upon this disclosure; like John and Michael, they have for the most part gotten on well.

John goes on to talk about the early years of Smith Printing, when he and Dorothy sometimes worked night and day to meet deadlines for high-quality products. As he talks, Rob and Kathy look at their parents with a new appreciation for their self-sacrifice and cooperation during those years.

Kathy raises a point that none of them had thought of in years: the younger Smiths joined Smith Printing in 1981, a recession year when soaring interest rates and paper costs were threatening the survival of the business. Though no one talked much about it at the time, the whole family tacitly understood that the children's contribution had probably made the difference between survival and demise for Smith Printing.

"If we got through that together, I guess we can survive this," John says. Initially surprised that John would compare the family's current problems with that near-disastrous time, the rest of the family thoughtfully agrees.

The consultant suggests that the children's contribution not be underestimated. Just as Frank Jr. saved the family farm in the Depression, Rob and Kathy helped save the family business from recession — in Rob's case, at the cost of a major change in career plans.

The Father-Son Legacy. As the family grows more comfortable with the discussion, the consultant asks John about his cutoff from his father. John recalls that while Frank Jr. liked to experiment with progressive farming techniques, he was conservative on issues of family duty and inheritance. He bore a firm and unquestioned expectation that his oldest son would take over the farm, beginning at age 18. He never discussed the idea with John.

All the while, John was trying to contain a growing sense of adventure. While he enjoyed working with machinery on the farm — an aptitude that would serve him well in the printing business — he longed for a new opportunity of his own. The farm didn't seem to him to afford much chance to exercise creativity or enterprise. While his mother heard John's wishes and seemed to understand, his father simply didn't listen. Sadness is evident on John's face as he talks.

Rob is dumbstruck. With a few words changed, John's story could be his own. Just as his own father did, John has made a decision about Rob's future without consulting Rob. With a flash of compassion, Rob sees for the first time that his father is not even aware that he is treating his son in the same way he himself was treated. And he feels a sense of kinship with his father that he has not felt in a long time.

What would it have taken for John to commit to the farm, the consultant asks. "If my brother hadn't been there to take over, I never could have left," John replies. "Michael is a capable guy, and I knew Mom and Dad would be all right."

"What would have happened to Michael if you had stayed?" the consultant asks.

John pauses, then says, "We would have had to try to work together. And there just wasn't enough to go around. That farm wasn't big enough to support two families."

"Did your father realize that?" the consultant asks.

"I don't think he had time to give it any thought," John says. "He had to take over the farm when he was a kid, and I think he just expected me to do the same. I don't think he thought beyond that."

"Sounds as though you did your family a favor by leaving. You solved a future problem that your father hadn't even anticipated," the consultant says.

"I guess I did," John says, after a pause. He fell silent as the discussion turned to other subjects.

John's insight began a process of healing a wound that, without his realizing it, still affects his family relationships. John now will likely find it much easier to be more flexible in his plans for Rob and Kathy as well.

John's and Dorothy's Plans for Retirement. Like most families, the Smiths have a large number of forebears who died before or near retirement. John's grandfather Frank Jr. died working, and Dorothy's parents died within a year of each other, just after her father retired. While this pattern is not unusual, it has helped make Dorothy anxious about the future and reluctant to engage in retirement planning. She may wonder if John's retirement portends the end of their years together. Avoiding the issue may ease these fears for Dorothy.

As the family discusses the meaning of retirement in the Smith clan, however, they find a model of success: John's Uncle Alan and his wife Mattie, who enjoyed more than a decade of retired happiness together, travelling and doing charitable work. As John recalls some of the family jokes about Alan and Mattie's septuagenarian escapades in Las Vegas, Europe and elsewhere, he and Dorothy both grow excited about their prospects. Dorothy agrees to begin researching travel plans for the two of them.

John recalls that Alan also ran the city's United Way chapter for two years, and Mattie did volunteer work in neighborhood schools. Like Alan and Mattie, the consultant suggests, John and Dorothy may need more than travel to occupy them after retirement. With his encouragement, they agree to discuss some possibilities for meaningful projects.

As the consultant points out, focusing on Alan and Mattie's example may also make it easier for John to hand over management authority and responsibility in the family business. Though his conscious dream always has been to pass on a business legacy to his children, unconscious fears of retirement sometimes make this goal unexpectedly hard for business owners to reach.

The Strength of the Nuclear Family. The Smith family genogram is remarkable in that it contains no evidence of divorce, extramarital affairs or other disharmony. This observation by the consultant prompts some talk about the closeness of nuclear families in the Smith clan. Dorothy recalls how much she appreciated her father's always being home for dinner with the family. Kathy remembers how she relied on her parents for advice as a child, and Rob even volunteers that he was proud of his parents' loyalty to each other amid a rash of divorces among his friends' families.

"That raises some questions," the consultant says. On a spectrum, the Smiths tend to be more enmeshed than disengaged, he observes, and an abrupt shift toward disengagement could be uncomfortable for them all. "Without the family business keeping you together in your day-to-day activities, will the family need other ways of staying in close touch? If Smith Printing is 'the linchpin of the family's life,' as John has said, what will serve as the family glue in the future?"

The consultant suggests some ways other families have used to maintain family traditions, values and closeness, including family meetings, family-history or education projects and family retreats. John and Dorothy agree to do some planning for family activities after John's retirement — an effort, the consultant points out, that could give both of them a much-needed sense of continuity through this difficult phase.

The Role of Women in the Family. Another family pattern, the consultant notes, is the prominent role of women in family enterprises. As he asks John to talk about his grandmother Anna and his mother Alice, Rob and Kathy listen intently. John's estrangement from Frank Jr. has kept them from knowing their paternal grandparents well, and they are intensely curious.

Some of John's earliest memories of Alice, he recalls, are of her working around the farm while he toddled behind. He remembers riding his tricycle while she unloaded wagons of grain and playing by the fire while she worked on the farm books in the evenings. After he went to bed, John remembers falling asleep to the muted tones of her voice drifting through the door of his bedroom, discussing yields, profits or planting plans with his father.

For the first time, Alice takes shape in Kathy's consciousness as a model of a strong woman who combined work and family throughout her life. After a pause, the consultant turns to Kathy with a smile. "It looks as though women's combining work and family isn't an entirely new thing in your family, Kathy," he says.

"Here I thought I was a pioneer," Kathy laughs. After a pause, she adds thoughtfully, "Actually, I haven't even begun to address some of those issues — like how do you have kids when you're trying to help run a business?"

Seeing her anxiety, Ken breaks in, "You talk as if these kids are your sole responsibility. Don't we have to work on this together?"

Kathy joins the rest of the family in laughter, then adds, "I guess these are things I...*we*... should be thinking about now — as part of this transition."

Putting New Insights to Work. For the Smiths, the discussions around the genogram reopen communication channels and serve as a starting point for a series of new planning and problem-solving efforts.

■ Realizing that he is unintentionally recreating with Rob the kind of situation that drove him to cut himself off from his father, John looks for ways to communicate with his son about plans for his future and the future of the business. John is likely to find this particularly difficult, since he never experienced this kind of communication with his own father.

He wants Rob to feel free to make an independent commitment to the firm. He, Rob and Kathy begin a series of meetings with the consultant during which they struggle with the plans and decisions necessary to balance each of their needs. John hopes that each child will take on the responsibilities of ownership and feel free to implement new ideas. On the other hand, he finds himself much less tolerant of risk-taking as he and Dorothy work on their financial needs for retirement.

John realizes that Rob may decide to leave management and remain with the family business only as an owner. While John would find that difficult, he strongly prefers it to losing touch with his son altogether.

■ As John tries to develop positive ways to pass on the business, he decides with the consultant's encouragement to try to reestablish contact with his brother Michael. He realizes that he knows almost nothing about how his father turned the farm over to Michael after he left. He wonders whether his father did anything in particular that Michael found helpful or harmful. Perhaps, John reasons, he can still learn something from his father's example. For the first time in 41 years, he makes plans to attend the annual family reunion at the farm in Indiana.

■ John reflects on all the issues raised by the family discussion and decides his retirement warrants a broader planning effort. He needs to focus on planning his own post-retirement role in the business. He needs to develop a financial plan to sustain him and Dorothy after retirement, in addition to an estate plan. Even more worrisome for John, the business needs an updated strategic plan, an effort that has stalled in the hands of Rob and Kathy.

- Dorothy begins planning regular family meetings and reunions to preserve family closeness after John's retirement. As she returns to her projects with the community library, she finds herself wondering how the process of her retirement will proceed. If Rob does not marry, will the task of organizing family events fall on Kathy's shoulders, and will this be too much for her? She is pleased to see Rob working with the consultant on alternative ways of meeting his personal goals while fulfilling his responsibilities to Smith Printing. On the other hand, she finds herself remaining very sensitive to any plans that would take him farther from home. Conscious of the problems created by triangles, she works with the consultant to state her concerns in the family meetings and to ask each of the children about their expectations for family connection.

- Rob needs to do some serious self-analysis about his goals for himself, the business and the family. His inner conflict is real and significant. Whether he can meet his needs and goals within the family business is a question that needs to be addressed openly and honestly before he can make any expanded commitment to the business.

- Rob and Kathy are relieved by their parents' commitment to be more open about their expectations and to listen to their children's perspectives. While brother and sister find that some of the tension between them has disappeared, during continuing discussions they continue to struggle with some of the real differences in style and strategy between them. For them, experimentation with alternative ways of resolving their differences becomes an important challenge. They are most satisfied with their brainstorming successes when they discover new perspectives that combine each of their strengths.

- Kathy begins to face some tough potential conflicts, including the issue of how her plans to have children would mesh with her expanded responsibilities in the business. She weighs a variety of options, from hiring live-in help to temporarily deferring her new responsibilities at work.

VII. *How Transitions Raise Family Issues*

As the Smiths have discovered, any transition that brings a reorganization of the family, the business or both can lead to tension or conflict in even the most peaceful families.

Business crises, deaths, economic downturns, divorce and other "structural" changes are highly likely to create situations in which an understanding of how families work can be particularly helpful.

The death of a member of the parent generation, reading of a will or sharing an estate plan can raise questions about fairness and expectations of individual family members. The firing of a family member from the business, or even discussions about holding a family meeting or setting up a trust, also can trigger family unrest.

Issues that seem to affect only the business can expose longstanding family feelings. Reorganizing the board of directors, for instance, can spark discussions about the rights of family members, bringing to the surface feelings rooted in childhood. The transition from a parent leader to a son or daughter as successor can stir deep-seated resentments about the allocation of power in the family.

Once a new generation takes control, another set of family issues that may have been avoided in the past can be exposed. Members of the second generation of family owners, for instance, may by consensus agree to take the reins of the family company. But once the older generation is no longer present as a calming influence, the new leaders may feel a need to resolve conflicts and resentments that they have suppressed over the years. The impulse to "clear the air" or "put it all on the table" may create a tense, complex situation that requires the presence of a facilitator for a smooth resolution.

Integrating In-Laws. Integrating in-laws is among the most challenging structural changes for many business families.

In some families, in-laws are blamed for a range of family-business troubles. They are criticized for complaining too much or for being ill-informed about the business. In fact,

> *Integrating in-laws is among the most challenging structural changes for many business families.*

57

in-laws usually hear only what their spouses choose to tell them about the business, so they can hardly be blamed for having a one-dimensional perspective. Also, they become as much a part of the family system as anyone, serving as a mouthpiece for the frustrations of a spouse or a focal point for the problems of a parent.

Business families may attract as in-laws people who desire the positive, constructive energy they generate. Because of family members' energy and cohesiveness, their family gatherings and fun may fill some gaps lingering from an in-law's childhood. There is nothing wrong with this pattern. The in-law may benefit from a long-sought sense of family, and both the family and the business may benefit from the in-law's presence. And the older generation of family-business managers may be delighted at the advent of a talented new family member, particularly if the in-law's skills fill gaps in management.

If in-laws are to be integrated effectively, though, both the in-law and the family need to be explicit about the relationship. That requires the business-owning family to answer some questions up front: Do we want to make the in-law part of the family or not? Do we have enough confidence in that person's relationship with our family member to invest in a relationship with the in-law? Do we want to afford the in-law any family privileges, such as access to a job in the business, or to ownership? How should we educate the in-law about the business?

From the family's perspective, this soul-searching may translate into written policies. This enables the family to weigh complex issues in a calm and constructive context rather than in crisis. The policies should answer such questions as: What would happen to an in-law working in the business if a divorce occurs? Should we have employment policies that ban in-laws from working in the business? Can in-laws succeed to family-business leadership, including the CEO slot? Can in-laws own stock? If so, should we have buy-sell agreements in place in the event of divorce?

If the in-law is joining the business, the family also needs to think about his or her prospective relationships on the job with other family members. A son-in-law, for instance, should probably not be put in a position of supervising the owner's developing sons or daughters. Above all, the in-law should not be expected to do the

The in-law may benefit from a long-sought sense of family, and both the family and the business may benefit from the in-law's presence.

family's psychological "business" — disciplining errant offspring or becoming the perfect son the owner always wanted.

If these issues are not addressed, the in-law risks being let down if future decisions about authority and ownership in the business are guided by blood relationships (as they usually are). And parents run the risk of using the in-law, at least temporarily, as a stand-in for "the son (or daughter) we never had," thereby avoiding resolving their relationships with their own offspring. No matter how extraordinary the in-law's dedication or talent, it cannot heal a primary wound: a failed parent-child relationship. Such disappointments need to be addressed independent of relationships with others.

The in-law can play a major role in a family business without being a surrogate. **From the in-law's perspective, a first step toward healthy integration is to begin building individual relationships with family members from the ground up.** The in-law should get to know each member of the spouse's family in his or her own right. Triangles are to be avoided. If some tensions exist between the spouse and one or both of her parents or other family members, the in-law should avoid carrying messages.

VIII. *A Few Simple Rules for Smooth Family Functioning*

Here are a few more principles that, in our experience, have helped many business families:

- Develop a family code of conduct. (See Exhibit 3.)

- Hold family meetings. (See "Family Meetings: How to Build a Stronger Family and A Stronger Business," No. 2 in the **Family Business Leadership Series.**)

- Keep confidential all of your discussions about family patterns and behavior.

- Never undermine another family member in front of others.

- Talk directly, one on one, with all other family members — including those with whom you are not directly involved.

- Listen as well as talk.

- Work hard to find constructive ways to address conflict.

- Agree that it's OK to express feelings; consider the possibility that they may be valid signals of issues that need attention.

- View family harmony as a part of the family's overall mission in business together.

- Rather than trying to make your business more like a family, as many people suggest, families should be more like businesses, says psychologist Kenneth Kaye. "What a world this would be if we all treated each other as we do our most valued clients, employees, employers, customers and suppliers!" he says.

- Cultivate friends and interests outside the family, to lend perspective to your family dealings.

- Begin statements with "I," not "you." This encourages a constructive focus on one's own experience, rather than on criticizing or blaming others.

- Before losing your temper, ask yourself, "How would other members of the family feel about this issue?"

- Discuss family problems when you feel calm, not agitated or angry.

EXHIBIT 3

One Family's Code of Conduct

"Our family is fortunate to have as members people of differing personalities, skills, motivations and goals. Our diversity gives us strength, fosters creativity and permits various kinds of contributions. Despite any differences, we commit ourselves to each other. We will support each other and respond to family members' needs. We realize that conflicts will occur, but commit to compromise, planning, communication and love as to limit any injury conflict may cause. Conflicts will be less destructive if we maintain flexibility and openness to change. We will listen respectfully to all, young and old."

Excerpt from a family mission statement by a family moving into its fourth generation of shared business ownership.

- Don't carry messages for others. Instead, encourage them to speak and listen directly to each other.

- Don't ask others to carry messages for you. Talk directly to each other.

- Ask questions about what others feel and think. Don't interpret their viewpoint for them or assume that you already understand.

- Be explicit in your communications goals. If you want to have a real conversation instead of an argument, say so.

- In a discussion, state your own viewpoint — your interests and your needs, rather than your position or demand on the issue.

- Listen to and respect alternate viewpoints.

- Don't agree to a position you have reservations about without voicing the reservations.

- Focus on what you have in common, rather than what divides you. Make separate lists of goals and compare them to identify shared interests.

- Stick to the issues.

- Focus on goals rather than personalities.

- Avoid laying blame or making personal attacks.

- Pay attention to your own role in perpetuating a problem.

- Don't wait for the other guy to change first.

- Be aware of your own resistance to "letting go" of control over others, and be aware of how you hold on.

- Pay attention to your tensions, which may tell you when a family pattern or value is being threatened.

- Give positive feedback.

- Don't expect the business setting to offer emotional support. If it's there, consider it a bonus.

- Respect each other's space, individual differences, choice of spouses and other personal decisions.

Working on Communications Skills. Many families begin their work together by focusing on communications skills.

Some read books on effective communication and discuss them together. Other families invite speakers to family meetings to talk about communications issues. Still others may send family members to seminars, family business forums or courses in interpersonal communication. This learning can pay big dividends for the day-to-day workings of the business. (See Table 8.)

TABLE 8

SOME TIPS FOR
EFFECTIVE COMMUNICATION

1. Talk directly to the other person — not to someone else.

2. State your viewpoint and listen to the other person's as well.

3. Begin statements with "I," a technique to stick to expressing your own viewpoint and to avoid making judgmental, evaluative or accusatory remarks about others.

4. Repeat the other person's viewpoint as you heard it to make sure you understood it.

5. If any questions arise in your mind about what the other person meant, ask them.

6. Try to find common ground.

7. Use that common ground, rather than your differences, as a starting point.

8. Don't agree to a solution you can't live with.

9. When appropriate, put agreements in writing to avoid misunderstandings.

IX. *Some Signals That a Family May Be in Trouble*

Many business families are so accustomed to weathering hardships and challenges together that they assume they can get through almost anything.

Nevertheless, certain events or developments in our experience have tended to signal family troubles in need of attention, in some cases professional attention.

For the Smiths, an early warning signal was the family's inability to have an open, mutual discussion at that first family meeting. Here is a sampling of other trouble signs:

- Frequent arguments.

- A failure to resolve many arguments.

- No arguments at all.

- No discussions of important issues.

- Symptoms in a family member, such as depression or other stress-related problems.

- Loss of a customary sense of fun or humor.

- Avoidance of family meetings.

- Family meetings where nothing is accomplished.

- Family members' acting in hurtful or damaging ways to one another.

- The cutoff of one family member.

Families often deny the significance of the cutoff of one member from important family events or functions. They may say, "Well of course we would like to see that person reunited with the family, but she will never change." They may assign her departure from the fold to reasons unique to her, having no significance to themselves.

Though a detailed discussion of this issue is beyond the scope of this booklet, an individual's cutoff is generally a symptom of a family dynamic. Most people prefer to be connected to their families; it is a near-instinctive drive toward collective association with the people, rituals and legacy that created us. **Thus when one family member cuts himself or herself off, the reason likely arises from the way the family system is functioning.**

X. The Role of the Family Professional

When trouble arises, some families find it helpful to bring in family business professional, such as a consultant, an organizational psychologist, or a trained therapist or counselor with an understanding of family business.

John Smith wisely sought help to shed perspective on the family's problems very early in the succession process, before any major difficulties developed. Some families consult professionals even earlier, when they realize they are approaching a potentially stressful reorganization. While consultants can aid in solving problems, they also can help families to avoid them.

In some cases, several family members may agree to engage in counseling to tackle family-systems questions together. Family consensus is extremely powerful. If everyone can agree on even one thing — to consult a professional for guidance and insights — chances of resolving other difficulties are high. Paradoxically, the outside help will likely play a smaller role in that resolution than the family's simple willingness to work together — and to admit that things need to change.

Families at this stage should be aware of the distinction between the consultant and the therapist. Each can serve as a valuable resource to business families. A consultant acts as an advisor, problem-solver or facilitator to the family business. He or she is oriented to completing certain tasks with specific goals in mind. The consultant may meet privately or in a group with family members. But the focus is on the interplay of family and business issues.

While a knowledge of family therapy can be helpful to a consultant, he or she does not practice therapy. For instance, a couple in business together might seek a consultant's help with specific management problems like working out a constructive balance between differing styles, balancing out their roles at work and at home, or plans to encourage their children to enter the business. But if they decide they want to work on personal problems between them, they should be referred to a therapist — preferably one with a knowledge of family business.

The therapist's role is that of working with a family or its individual members to achieve personal growth. The therapist tries to help equip and empower the individual, or the family as a group, to solve their own problems. He or she focuses on that process of understanding and transformation as it relates to emotional pain and stress in intimate relationships. In therapy, the client has broad latitude; any personal concerns and issues may surface in therapy sessions, whether or not they relate to the business.

While some family-business professionals are qualified to play both the therapist's and the consultant's roles, it is difficult to do both simultaneously.

Professional help is clearly needed in cases where alcohol or other substance abuse has arisen. While dealing with alcohol or drug dependency is beyond the scope of this booklet, business families grappling with this issue frequently rely on professional treatment programs. And many find it wise to establish policies for dealing with problems *before* any problems arise.

Outside help will likely play a smaller role in that resolution than the family's simple willingness to work together — and to admit that things need to change.

Summary

Families in business together share a rich blend of experience and history that can empower or encumber them — and their business. Long-standing family patterns of behaving and relating to each other are woven deeply into family members' legacy. These unconscious patterns can surface with great force, particularly in times when the family or the business is being restructured.

A growing number of business owners are acknowledging the powerful relationship between business and family and working to integrate the two in the most productive way possible. For many, this means building a greater understanding of how families work. Learning together about family dynamics can create new synergies that benefit both the business and the family. Family self-study can cultivate tolerance, empathy and humor. It also can help change problem behaviors, which often are rooted in the unconscious family patterns of the past. The best way to rob these patterns of their potentially negative power is to recognize and learn about them.

This booklet discusses some of the characteristics of normal families and how they interact, particularly under stress. Conflict, criticism and communications failures are all part of these families' experience. But in normal families, negative communications are accompanied by frequent positive, constructive exchanges. Relationships thrive on honest, explicit communication. Normal families strive for a balance between flexibility and stability. Power is shared and cooperation is stressed. Feelings are accepted and shared. Members enjoy negotiating with each other, and agreement results from inventive compromise.

Principles of family systems theory, a body of thought that holds that the family is an emotionally meaningful unit with its own dynamics, can be helpful in understanding the workings of one's own family. These concepts — differentiation of self, triangling, birth order, sibling rivalry and emotional cutoff — are familiar dimensions of every family's day-to-day life together. Some families construct a genogram — an information-rich format for drawing a family tree — to help them identify multi-generational patterns of behavior and experience in their own families.

Family self-study can cultivate tolerance, empathy and humor.

All families, no matter how well-adjusted, experience some problems. The structural changes that are a part of life — death, succession, business crises, economic downturns, divorce and so on — can bring a pileup of stresses that raise major family issues. Family professionals can be helpful, either in anticipating such changes or in adapting to them when they arise.

Suggested Reading List

Aronoff, Craig A., and John L. Ward. *Family Meetings: How to Build a Stronger Family and a Stronger Business*, **The Family Business Leadership Series**, No. 2. Marietta, GA: Business Owner Resources, 1992.

Bowen, Murray. *Family Therapy In Clinical Practice*. New York: Aronson, 1978.

Friedman, Stewart D., "Sibling Relationships and Intergenerational Succession in Family Firms," *Family Business Review*. San Francisco: Jossey-Bass Inc., Spring 1991.

Herz, Fredda. *Reweaving the Family Tapestry: A Multigenerational Approach to Family*. New York: Norton & Co., 1991.

Lewis, J. S., and others. *No Single Thread: Psychological Health in Family Systems*. New York: Brunner/Mazel, 1976.

McGoldrick, Monica, and Randy Gerson. *Genograms in Family Assessment*. New York: W. W. Norton & Co., 1985.

Minuchin, Salvadore. *Families and Family Therapy*. Cambridge, MA: Harvard University Press, 1974.

Index

The Authors

Mary F. Whiteside, Ph.D. is a family therapist, consultant and mediator affiliated with the Ann Arbor Center for The Family. She holds a Ph.D. in clinical psychology from the University of Michigan and served as a faculty member there for ten years.

A practitioner member of the Academy of Family Mediators has contributed significantly to the introduction of family system concepts to the family business field. Her publications and presentations include numerous articles about families in family businesses and about families experiencing divorce and remarriage.

Craig E. Aronoff, Ph.D. is a co-founder and principal of The Family Business Consulting Group, Inc.®, a leading consultant, speaker, writer, and educator in the family business field.

As the founder of the Cox Family Enterprise Center at Kennesaw State University in Marietta, GA, Aronoff invented and implemented the membership-based, professional-service-provider sponsored Family Business Forum, which has served as a model of family business education for some 150 universities world-wide. Until his retirement in 2005 from the university, he held the Dinos Eminent Scholar Distinguished Chair of Private Enterprise and was a professor of management in Kennesaw State's Coles College of Business.

As a consultant, Aronoff has worked with hundreds of family companies in the U.S. and abroad on issues including generational transitions; developing business and family governance processes and structures; finding and articulating family missions and values; facilitating decision making and conflict resolution; managerial development; family compensation and dividend policies; family meetings; and more. As an inspiring, informative and entertaining speaker on a variety of family business topics, he speaks regularly to trade and professional groups and has lectured at over one hundred universities.

With co-author John L. Ward, Aronoff is perhaps the most prolific writer in the family business field. He has authored, co-authored or been editor of more than two dozen books, including many of the titles in the *Family Business Leadership Series* and is executive editor of *The Family Business Advisor*.

Listed in *Who's Who* and widely acknowledged for his work in the area of family business, Aronoff has received, among other honors: the Family Firm Institute's Beckhard Award for Outstanding Contributions to Family Business Practice; The Freedom Foundation's Leavey Award for Excellence in Private Enterprise Education; and the National Federation of Independent Business Foundation's Outstanding Educator Award.

Aronoff grew up in a family business. He received his bachelor's degree from Northwestern University, his Masters from the University of Pennsylvania, and his Doctorate from the University of Texas at Austin.

John L. Ward, Ph.D. is a co-founder of The Family Business Consulting Group, Inc.®, clinical professor at Kellogg School of Management and Wild Group Professor of Family Business at IMD. Ward teaches strategic management, business leadership and family enterprise continuity. He is an active researcher, speaker and consultant on family succession, ownership, governance and philanthropy.

He is the author of many leading texts on family business including, *Keeping the Family Business Healthy*, *Creating Effective Boards for Private Enterprises*, *Strategic Planning for the Family Business* and *Perpetuating the Family Business: 50 Lessons Learned from Long-Lasting Successful Families in Business*. He is also co-author of a collection of booklets, *The Family Business Leadership Series*, each focusing on specific issues family businesses face.

Ward graduated from Northwestern University (B.A.) and Stanford Graduate School of Business (M.B.A. and Ph.D.). He is the co-director of The Center for Family Enterprises at Kellogg and currently serves on the boards of several companies in the U.S. and Europe. He conducts regular seminars in Spain, Italy, India, Hong Kong, Sweden, and Switzerland.

John and his wife, Gail, a Chicago high school principal, live in Evanston, Illinois. They have two adult children. They are active in community and educational activities and enjoy family travel and sports.